Animal Instincts

Also by Steve Evans

Poetry
Adult Fiction
Algebra
Bonetown
Edison Doesn't Invent the Car
Luminous Fruit
Taking Shape
Unearthly Pleasures
Useful Translations

Fiction
Easy Money and Other Stories

Non-fiction
Balancing Act: The Creative Writing Pathway to Understanding Accounting (with Lee Parker)
Best of Friends: the first 30 years of the Friendly Street Poets (with Kate Deller-Evans)
Lift Off! an introductory course in creative writing (with Kate Deller-Evans)

As Editor
Another Universe (with Kate Deller-Evans)
Corridors: Words on the Ward (with Kate Deller-Evans)
Lament – Michèle St Yves
New Poets 20
New Poets 21
New Poets 22
Ochre 10
synonym for sobriety – Ben Adams

Steve Evans

Animal Instincts

Acknowledgements

Some poems in this collection, or earlier versions of them, appeared in *Burrow, The Crow, Effective Living, Friendly Street Reader No. 41, Infinite Dirt* and *Patterns of Living*.

My thanks to Arts South Australia through which the South Australian Government provided financial support via a Barbara Hanrahan Fellowship to enable a draft of this book to be completed.

Animal Instincts
ISBN 978 1 76109 508 5
Copyright © text Steve Evans 2023
Cover image: used with the kind permission of Judith Nangala Crispin – https://www.facebook.com/jude.crispin

First published 2023 by
GINNINDERRA PRESS
PO Box 3461 Port Adelaide 5015
www.ginninderrapress.com.au

Contents

We	9
Birds & Bees	
Beginning	13
Farm Swallows	15
The Hardware Store Cockie	16
A Clockwork Rooster	17
Darlings	18
Magpies	19
Bumblebee	20
The Book of Crow	21
The Coming of the Bees	28
A Blackbird Looks Back	29
The Lyre is Dead	33
The Love of Birds	34
The Next Rough Creature	
Snails, She Said	37
Possum Song	38
Sprung	40
Fish Light	42
Fox	43
Cockroach, Honey	44
Forest Creature	45
Circles	46
Cats & Dogs	
Raining Cats	49
The Right Dog	50
Sun Cat Earth	51
The God of Cats	52
Shooting the Dogs	53

Cat Poetry	54
By Morning	55
Dog / Cloud	56
Catt Goes Out	57
The Knack	59
Cushion	61
The Lie	62
Cat's Eye	63
Sirens	64

Sex & Camouflage

The First Blowfly of Spring	67
The Quick Brown Fox	68
Ants	69
Wrestling, with Liberace	70
Markings	71
After Sex	72
Stick Insect	73
Mousing	74
Fish Memoir	75
No Animals	76

Burning Tigers

Painting Tigers	79
Tiger	80
Tigers I Used to Be	82

Bent Wolf

Rumour	87
I, Wolf	88
The Wolf and Veil Song	89
Wolf Light	90
Territory	91
Winter Night	92

Bird Hunting	93
Other Voices	94
The Heart of It	95
Calling	97
Taking Bait	98
Where the End	99
Wolf (Not Wolf)	100
The New Animal Speaks	102

We

We sing your startled world awake,
brash outside your window.

We chew through your pantry packets,
connoisseurs of cardboard and cereals.

We decimate your best roses,
beautiful in our hunger and appetite.

We hang suspended in a clear shoal,
hypnotic and hypnotised.

We burrow beneath your houses.
Your floorboards are delicious.

We wear wings briefly before dying.
This is not for joy or your pity.

We flirt with twilight air,
gorging on a host of midges.

We enjoy your blood.
Not so much the slapping and poisons.

We quarrel in treetops,
arguing the sun's decline.

We sleep at the foot of your bed.
Your company is ours, not vice versa.

We scuttle under cupboards,
avoiding traps and torchlight.

We are not what you suppose
and never will be.

If most of you forget about us,
that's the way we like it best.

Birds & Bees

Beginning

Bird Says

In the beginning was Bird.
We clevered air, confused it,
skyrunning its restless mind.
We fooled air
with slicing and coasting,
swimming its anger and sleep,
surfing its uncertainties.

Time made us, needle bones
and a stitching of feathers,
for toys, displays,
but now we call each day into being.
The first voice you hear is ours.
We are time.
We made it.

They Say

In the beginning was Bird?
That's what all the boast birds sing –
their daily chorus claiming first and last word.
Fish say they were earlier,
though their record-keeping's woeful.
Snakes insist with constant hiss
that they created God, so well before
God's own claim existed.

Who to believe, if anyone –
fish, fowl or invertebrate?
I favour the quietest,
the least outspoken, mouthless one
that floated in on a cosmic wind
without ambition of any kind –
an accidental tourist for whom
there was no Welcome sign
or immigration shack,
no stamp to be stamped
and no possible sending back.

Farm Swallows

Their nest was a fist of dry twigs
and grass in the rafters –
its spotted apron of shit spread out
below the song of an unseen brood.

The passing weeks soon saw
three young swallows circle in the shed –
three satellites risking an orbit
fixed as a stone swung on a string,
then growing full of dart and swerve in
twittering laps of the tin rectangle,
rounding off its corners
as rain tympani'd the roof.

The broken window their private door,
a gap slightly more than bird-size
through which they tucked their wings in flight
to test the outer world.
But when they had the beautiful ease of it,
the cat waited by the glassy crack
and batted them down
one by one
as they flew home.

The Hardware Store Cockie

The sulphur-crested cockatoo
high in the cavernous store
flexes his white serrated wing,
far above lock and hinge,
hacksaw and other hand tools.

Beneath his dark eye,
that glossed bead,
shoppers pause with weedkiller or axe,
hammer and drill bits,
packets of seeds,
to watch him watching them
from that sheened and sideways limb,
that untrue tree.

He tilts his head and shivers,
squawking raucous.
His millennial call
speaks back through disappeared forests,
creeks that were here
beneath the flocks that dinned
long before buildings.

But he is only one,
stranded in the DIY section
well beyond any ladder or cunning,
admired on his distant perch
until he works out his own exit
at closing time.

A Clockwork Rooster

Tiny wheels inside me
drive my roosterness along.
I'm all spindles and cogged specifics,
diameter and radius,
beautifully engineered.
My feathers are shone metal.
Wings' lovely robotics shudder with precision.
My red comb rises just like a real one does.

My call is set to loud enough.
My standard deviation's nil.
I'm perfection in a bird.
A jealous crow is watching me
from a fence rail but
if I'm cocksure, it's justified.
I'm in lockstep with the sun.
I am the world's most glorious alarm.

You should hear me cry.
Mad as a comet's tail,
I strut without strut,
revolve on this rooftop,
sending daylight in a fanfare
to those who wake or won't.
And I don't care
where the other rooster went.

Darlings

Bees are so precise.
Mini-machines with tiny engines a-whirr,
they are crusted jewellery,
live ornaments of bustle and maybe,
jigging preciously between dalliances –
this flower, that. Such flirts.

The garden's darlings
have no time for their own beauty.
You could put one on your lapel
and sex your fingers
with excess pollen in the process,
but at your own risk.
There's the catch, the sting.
Better just to watch.

Magpies

Never mind the melodies, the constant carolling.
I'm not saying your liquid sound isn't pretty,
if a little drunken,
it's just that your attire doesn't suit.
You look like you dressed for the party in a hurry,
with your tuxedos on backwards.

Your shirtfronts are brilliant white,
but they face to the rear.
Your coal-black coats reversed as well.
Is this meant to confuse
or are you mocking us?

Gathering at the end of the street,
your gang of eight or nine rehearses,
warming up for evensong.
I listen to the lilting rounds that come
like waterfalls exchanging gifts,
and know that you don't care for dress at all.

Bumblebee

It's Uncle Clarry
visiting on Sundays,
his fat tweed jacket and yellow vest
as he hovers between our old round couch
and the sherry parked on the sideboard.

Or it's the big swimmer in striped bathers
who crawls the last lane at the pool
for hours each afternoon,
inelegant and never effortless,
pushing on always to end at the beginning.

Now this tuft of wool and cellophane,
a haywire mini-jumbo jet,
lifts off into its own slow drone,
into a confusion of sunlight
and summer's intoxicated air.

Goodbye, Clarry,
Goodbye, swimmer,
Goodbye, bumblebee,
completing your laps in your Sunday best
and flying home haphazardly.

The Book of Crow

On the First Day

On the first day,
Crow created Crow in its own image
and was satisfied.

Crow doesn't have time for gossip.
Crow is a machine for solving
the problem of too much food.

Even the youngest Crow
has a thousand-year stare
that reads your discomfort precisely.

The skull of Crow is small
but it is a library of every animal,
all weather, the stark plenty of the world.

There is no God of Crows.
but if there were,
Crow would not believe in it.

Crow has constellations above,
the smallest insect below.
What need of gods?

A Story of Crow

Crow opens to where the story is about Crow.
Crow, here, is beautiful ink signing the sky.
Crow makes the rest of the world seem brighter.
Crow can recall every mouse it has seen.
Crow's dark humour is best kept for Crows.

Crow is a creature of its own devise.
Crow cannot be caught by lightning.
Crow taught lightning to dance.
Crow is blacker than the family Bible.
Crow has a High Street tailor make its outfits.

Crow preaches sermons on the virtues of Crow.
Crow prays at the altar of new death.
Crow is the blade for the bone that calls to it.
Crow knows the eyes of lambs see it last.
Crow sits on top of the world.

Crow on Fire

Outwardly, Crow is
lacquered as if still wet,
a fine Chinoiserie,
but Crow has heat beyond
its singularity.

At first no light escapes.
Crow is its own black hole
swallowing the smallest glimmer
of itself back into darkness,
into the space of Crow.

But it burns.
Crow is on fire within,
a small, delicate flame
the size of a bird's heart
in its engine room.

You might see it
when two or three together
glow in their bleak joy,
jointly glistening
the meaning of Crow.

Crow's Sunday Service

Though he thinks he's a sharp dresser,
        Crow is tatty today.
He clenches his fine claws
        tighter on the wire.
The drops of gone rain
        are small jewels all about him.

Down there on the wet ground
        is a meagre house
with an old woman inside
        whose speech has abandoned her.
He thinks he sings her voice now,
        though he keeps this to himself.

Crow will tidy his frock coat
        and drop to her sill,
one of all things beautiful and bright,
        however dark, unkempt,
with his orison ready
        for a few stale crumbs of bread.

Crow and Shadow

Crow takes its shadow
to a spot beside the road.
Crow says to shadow,
'Here is where our meal will fall.'
But night comes with its darkness
and indifferent stars.
Crow sees that it is all alone.

In the morning sunlight,
when shadow has returned,
it asks, 'Where is our promised dinner?'
Crow only shakes its head
and then, forgetting grace,
eats its shadow at a gulp.
There was nothing else to do.
Sometimes you take what you can get.

Fox and Crow

I have a pelt of unimaginable beauty,
says Fox.
I am style and fire in motion.
        Crow does not speak.

I am a loner, free of my leash,
says Fox.
I am the glamour and the glory.
        Crow does not speak.

I see the Earth's magnetic field,
says Fox.
It feeds me, praises me.
        Crow does not speak.

I made the Northern Lights,
says Fox.
My tail swept sparks into the sky.
        Crow does not speak.

Fox settles on its paws,
twitches its famous ears,
and waits.
        Crow does not speak.

Crow tilts its head,
extends the dark fans of its wings,
and flies high above the dwindling red figure
without once looking down.

No Crow

Absences.
Outlines in the sky
where their darkness was.

Where ten of them might gather,
each one its own night,
now only the lack of Crow.

What will Crow mean
in the shadowed stories,
if we still speak them at all?

How will we tell our children
the time of Crow,
its before and after,

when Crow is gone,
in that no-Crow time?

The Coming of the Bees

Always we were told
        their disappearance
               was imminent,
their absence beyond doubt,
        with the usual habitats wasted,
              disease reducing their numbers.
An augury –
        the failure of our planet's
              vegetation in their wake.

Reports were dismissed then
        of the coming of the bees
              in remote places,
swarms moving into farmhouses,
        filling them entirely
               with giant hives,
valleys humming with the industry
        of millions of small bodies
              migrated from cities.

Their billowing waves began
        washing back into the suburbs,
              dark and alive
and searching for new food
        like one huge animal
               asserting its domain.
We woke to carpets of bees,
        bees turning trees to their tune,
              growing masses of bees, waiting.

A Blackbird Looks Back

1

You
wingless
poor soul that no air buoys

Land wretch
crawler of earth –
looking skyward will do you no good

II

I music me
make stillness
darker than the purple dark
of the storm front
fizzing its fierce
electrical
possibilities

III

One this / each one
in its dialect
singular as every now
of sudden
tipped flight
speaks me fluently

IV

Not the quiet before her anger
nor the emptiness after
but the small shadowed lull between
each knife-whetting plaint

V

VI

I am my geometry
silhouette of triangles
intersection of eye and sky
a point high in summer heat
over a stubbled field
that suspends from me –
in it is the small prey
that will have to move
eventually

VII

The glance she gives
you   over the restaurant
          table   after she says
it must end –
and the way her face shows
nothing

VIII

A certain configuration of us
arranged on the lawn
outside your door
is an ancient curse we utter
as a joke –
ah, but if we mean it?

IX

We are the dim assembly
grouped on this wire –
a gravity of blackbirds

X

We turned down blue
left that for the easy to please –
besides which
this sombre suit
suits us

XI

Were I you
I would fold my arms tight around myself
tuck my soft face into my chest
and dream feathers / beak / claws
the useless mantra
that at least makes you less
human
        for a while

XII

Awkward silence before
the monstrous freight of this
beautiful voice
black as angels' bitter ashes
fine as the shrill of train wheels –
beyond your primitive singing

XIII

Unlucky
for you
who are
not us

The Lyre is Dead

After the chainsaws left the valley
and there was nothing left to chop,
he sent us hammers and chainsaws,
a 'best of' album showcasing the easy cut,
the difficult one, and even the idling machine
before it set itself to another trunk.
He faithfully recorded his home
and its undoing,
along with sounds of other birds
and the truck horns he would replicate.

Those noises are gone now, just as he is,
taking the last of his language with him.
The trucks and the saws are elsewhere,
stripping the next valley, unmimicked there,
and doing their simple work without
his perfect pitch primed for instant replay.
His work is lost, uncatalogued,
except sometimes as they start their distant din
when what I think comes to me is his own copy
with its odd mechanical eloquence.
But, no, our lyre is dead.

The Love of Birds

What it means, he cannot say.
He has not learnt a language for this
and fears he might.
What feelings are these?

He imagines it could be like
waking with wings
and a sky full of strange cousins
summoning,
a commotion wheeling around him.

He hesitates on a high ledge,
the sun warm on his feathering chest
and embraces the fall.
Whether to Heaven or oblivion,
only the disappearing seconds will tell.

The Next Rough Creature

Snails, She Said

Write a poem about snails, she said.
I don't know why she wanted one,
except maybe to get me out of my chair,
out of the house.
I could have declined
but I sat in the garden and observed them
in their dirt-coloured camouflage helmets,
their slow unmilitary parade.

She was thinking of mindfulness, I guess,
how a snail is busy being a snail
and not much else,
yet these few in their snailish commerce
were bustling snail-style,
rushing for all their worth.
and no one was asking them to write poems.

Possum Song

She stared red-eyed into my torch
when I found her last night,
a furred handbag
grey as the branch she clung to,
her disguise let down by the
inverted question mark of her tail,
a soft hook that hung below.

Past midnight the thud of her landing
is a muffled drumming overhead
like a full tank of water knuckle-struck,
then small paws skitter their curved cutlery,
scrabbling across roof tiles
to an insect delicacy
or away from the neighbour's cat.

Now the rain comes,
politely, on tiptoe,
and I hear three quick taps
as she lifts rhythmically from the roof,
into a tree and its overhanging limb,
a pocket gymnast looping towards
a hollowed warmth somewhere
between our bed and the clouded stars.

There's no hiss yet or raucous cries,
no marsupial peak hour
of rummaging in the ceiling,
or piss stains through the plaster.
Our possum is still glassy-eyed,
curious and cute –
a novelty that will not last.

Sprung

1. The Weekend House

According to the mouse
behind a bar of bathroom soap
that is no longer our soap
but his sweet feast,
this house is not ours, it's his.

In each drawer or cupboard
lies more evidence –
spilt packets, chewed cardboard,
and scores of shitty exclamations
littered darkly on the floor.

As I set the traps I feel
the tensioned spring of wire held back,
like a poem's final line –
this time with death in it.

2. Night to Day

But mouse is skitterkins, doesn't read poetry.
All night we try to settle, jump, then nestle,
startle again from the edge of sleep
each time the hallway sensor light
semaphores his quick forays.

Morning's restless night reveals
the traps' bare metal sheen,
untripped, licked clean some time
between his daring raids
across pillows, sheets, our arms and feet.

We timorous beasties see too late
the house was the trap the mouse had set,
and we had taken the bait.

Fish Light

Near the surface, it is all refractions.
The water shivers with light.
A school flashes its silver signature back at the sun
as scales bend the eye to brilliance
with a hint of rainbow.
But there is other light –
luminescence that goes as deep as blackness will.

There it is always night's long fall.
The lure seduces equally in
distraction and attraction.
There each tiny bio-torch sings
Come! See!
in a beautiful silent dialect,
and with a hunger for whatever audience
is smaller than its mouth.

Fox

The stink that death doused you with
had pulled at us for days,
its shifting traces blamed at first on the
dubious state of the drains
or possums sleeping in our roof.
We found nothing.

Meanwhile, you lay under a garden bush,
bejewelled with wasps –
your teeth a treasure of white beads
set in that pinched sneer,
your body's ragged orange now a dimming fire,
returning to a raw and unfleshed sketch
of the fox I saw in our road,
paws moving soft as brushes over a snare drum.

I find a rake and rubbish bag,
drag your scruffy pelt from the lavender bush,
wondering whether car or poison did the trick –
old age if you were lucky.
The wasps disperse to other riches.

Cockroach, Honey

They play country classics on this station,
she says, slowly scratching her damp neck
as I count moths on the screen.

She smells of the bitter stuff
we smear on our wrists to ward off the
biting insects at dusk.

Doesn't nobody ever want to
just roll in that stink of themselves and each
other like melted butter, she laughs.

I don't know how long we kept it going but
I finally say, you better put on your clothes,
and I pick up my keys.

Do I really have to?
There's a storm coming, she says,
and I get so sticky in this heat.

Let's stay a while and you tell me about
how I make your skin just sing but, first,
won't you kill that cockroach, honey?

Forest Creature

(After the painting by Philippa McMahon, 1995)

I'm outside but I'm also inside this,
a character woken in a curse.
What kind of brutal fairy tale
makes me a wolf in human clothing?

I scratch at fur that I don't have.
A crow alights beside me,
tilting its head in enquiry.
It knows something is amiss.

Once, I lined my lies up in a row
full of symbols –
fallen pinecones,
star and arrow, that same crow.

See me here, licked clean,
sleek in the coat of the animal I am not,
on all fours, though, and blessed –
poised for the next rough creature I will be.

Circles

The sly spiral down to see one's prey aslant
without being seen.

Rings on water's surface around a mouth's slight
puckering from beneath.

Unfathomable eyes on a peacock's train,
all-seeing, and blind.

The dog chasing its tail in carousel –
closer, never closer.

Cattle gathered about the fallen calf –
before their hours' slow dispersing.

All the circles stare, catching us in the cross hairs,
then dissolve.

Cats & Dogs

Raining Cats

That cat over there
a minute ago had a mouse in his jaw.
Now look at him
falling through puzzled air.
And me,
whiskers still wet with milk,
sailing down from what,
a mile above ground?

Who put us here –
Tabby, Persian, moggie, Manx?
Whose weird idea was this,
throwing us towards the earth?
We're all just toys of someone with
a bad god complex.

Who'd want a crowd of raining cats?
…and dogs?
It can pour poodles till Tuesday
as far as I'm concerned.
Hell, we're the ones who always
land on our feet.
But why bother with this test?
And who cares about dogs, anyway?

The Right Dog

There's craft in this, a gift,
an art to choosing
the right dog
in the pound.
My daughter can't decide.
It's finally the promised day but
it seems too much.

There's music in each,
keen as they dance from paw to paw –
except one dog that calmly raises its nose.
Who are you? my daughter asks.
That slow gaze returning says:
I am half of our future days.
The dog has made its choice.

Sun Cat Earth

The police station door opened
on autumn's chill
and the cat walked out.

It crossed my path and lay
at the edge of the pavement
in the only patch of sun.

Turn and twist and twist and turn,
it rolled its back on the warmer ground.
Dusty fur switched left right left
long after it seemed decent.

Who was I in the face of this unspoken finesse
to shape an empty hymn,
a gesture to the finer art of feline wallowing?

Though I wrote it down all the same,
it isn't telling anything
except sun, cat, earth.

The God of Cats

Top dog in gods is the god of cats.
Indifferent to other gods as they to her.
Indifferent, indeed, to any creature
that brings no offering.
She is the now, the centre, the all.

She washes herself in no one else's light
but the brilliance of her own entitlement.
Say praise, she does not purr
except to please herself.
Say curse, she hears some other god accused.

In that space between not-cat states
is the true godliness made purely of cats.
Which cat will say it is not so?
Which cat would forgo its due,
let alone listen to you?

Shooting the Dogs

After the first one fell,
the dogs knew
and split the compass,
slower than bullets
but low and difficult to track.

One,
stupid,
didn't follow the rest
over the hills.
It slunk under the tank stand
close by.

I'm under there with it,
anticipating.

Cat Poetry

It has a lot to do with sunlight,
the best places to lie in it,
and mice.
Not much about politics
or etiquette.

You might find a verse or two
about prowling rooftops
under a pearly moon,
offered up in a sour meow,
but they're still rare.

Mostly, the literary arts have been
deserted for sleep and sex
and the warm, sweet crunch
of smaller creatures going to God
via the blessing of their catty teeth.

By Morning

She's gone drinking.
What's a honky-tonkin' moment
between friends? she asked.
Gonna get ugly,
blue as a migraine.

Cats come by
and ask after her.
I look at the river.
Might as well query the stars.
She's dancing with strangers again.

Dogs howl on the corner.
I don't care much anymore –
just enough to break something
and leave the door open in case
she's home by dawn.

Dog / Cloud

From one angle as we drive,
the cloud in the fierce blue sky above Bellana
is a bounding West Highland white terrier,
though from any other aspect
it's likely just a cloud.

That afternoon, our dog,
sleeping on the back porch,
is from almost every angle
the West Highland white terrier that he is,
bar one from which he is a cloud,
exhausted, that has landed here to rest
after a long chase through the country sky.

Catt Goes Out

Catt got his time for bowl
and telling human a care as if
any matter more than eat and sleep
then the quick flicker over fences
when the moon calls to praise his royalty

Catt of cats where are you heading
in your worn finery and eye out
for competition and them tomfooleries
who better think better of it 'cos
you're so fine?

Catt got his tough eye on
down bottom of the street looking
for fight stuff or dare ya to try
and his ragged tail so high
none of them does

Catt does the strut like
he's king of the dust and suburbs
and walks the beat bigger than any
you can't tell him this goes for
any other cat to belong

Catt slows at the corner thinks
pride same as day before and this
rightly mine for catting along so fine
a night for Catt the King of Cats
to call his raggedy own

Then Catt go home after a check tour
of the neighbourhood staring down
the lesser ones and stinking up
a few rank fences for warning
or advertising his charms

Catt the only cat that is he
knows all the ways round here
and keep the rule that say
boss of what I survey
Catt the King and always king

The Knack

I steal dogs.
There's a knack to it.
I don't want them.
They don't want me.
I don't even like them.

You'd think mastiffs would be worst.
They're pussycats.
It's the little ones.
Molecules of maddening noise,
teeth and sheer anger
and I hate every last whiny little
high-pitched lord of the world
miniaturised monster bastard one of them,
but it's a living, right?
You do what you have to do.

I won't tell you about the schnauzer.
Who cares about the schnauzer?
That's all graveyards and slow death.
Forget it.
No schnauzer.

I used to know how it works.
Time. Light. All that.
But then there were the dogs
and life completely changed.
What's innocence?
You become someone else.
It's like a marriage really.
Anyway, it's better than nicking fish.

When I was young they were
tooth, hair, paw,
big voice, little voice,
sometimes claw.
I remember their shapes, their rackety voices,
every last ridiculous dog-shaped one of them,
but of course it would all end badly.

It was the Want ad, yes.
That slightly childish wording
as if written by a cat with a grudge,
but that would be too silly.
The dog bit was easy.
What mattered was afterwards.
Which dog? This dog.
And all the undoing.

Cushion

Cats know laziness is divine – Charles Simic

At the end of our bed,
having washed and rewashed herself,
the cat has finally sunk
into the circle of itself,
a furred cushion.

No, wait, that is a cushion.
the cat is over there
curled up on the chair,
purring itself towards cushionhood.

During the night
they will swap
or not, hard to tell –
one of them later waking anyway,
and waiting royally for food.

The Lie

I have heard them,
conspiring against us,
confiding to each other.
Their sneaky embellishments.
Their bolder claims and brags
designed to stay unheard behind
the public face of loyalty,
and everything signed off with the wink
implicit in that wagging tail.

Rescue dogs, guide dogs for the blind?
Guardians of our dangers and treasures too?
Don't believe it.
They're playing a long game.
Always plotting, in the next room,
sleeping at the end of your bed
with one eye on you and your family,
or outside in their kennels,
dreaming of wolf days.
Man's best friend has an agenda.

How they must laugh when they see
the way they have saturated the human life.
Images of them in our albums, on walls,
in our cameras, phones, purses and wallets.
You think they have no poker face?
They're playing with your head.
Never trust a happy dog.

Cat's Eye

Before you were human,
we lived on a midden, us two,
and sang for our supper.
We knew the roofs and fences like our skin
and where all the keys were hidden.

Now I'm the cat of the house,
sat here at the blue door.
King of the midnight opera,
heir to a fortune in mice.
Nobody knows what I know.

When I sing of the past, you look away,
catcalls and moonlight fading.
You've forgotten our feline ways
though when you sleep, I curl at your feet,
always with one eye open,
reciting the story we're both in,
keeping it ajar for your return.

Sirens

I envy them, dogs and sirens.
Each Friday the fire station tests its warning,
the canine choir sings the suburb high
and I long to join that rippling wash of sound,
stand out on the porch and raise my voice with them.

Sometimes late at night under the spell
of stellar harmonics and a fat white moon
I promise I'll chase my tail, then yours,
and we can chew bones in the backyard,
just take that open gate and run.

Who'll come chasing us? Who'd dare?
We'll be the sirens,
and who cares if the neighbours complain?
We won't stop till breakfast time
and another siren's wail.

Sex & Camouflage

The First Blowfly of Spring

Fresh from some delicious decay,
your fuzzy siren rides
a breeze into our house,
a buzz that turns
from distant conversation's hum
into a radio off-station, right here.

Dressed in your own inelegance
you are so Yes, an optimist,
a little zigzaggery diesel
and slow as a bovver boy.
You were steampunk before steam or punk.

What else? Noisy winged brooch,
clumsy engine of pure purpose.
You go, dark crumpled foil,
little black tin drum
sheened as kerosene,
telling me spring has arrived,
then off to spread the news.

The Quick Brown Fox

Jumps over the lazy dog
and circles it.

The quick brown fox slows down
and inspects the dog closely.

The quick brown fox takes typing lessons
while the lazy dog sleeps.

The quick brown fox surveys
the letters not left over and thinks.

The quick brown fox writes to the newspaper
bemoaning the recent state of dogs.

The quick brown fox writes its memoirs,
signs books at author readings.

The lazy dog, no underdog,
writes a counter narrative.

The quick brown fox slows down some more
and watches the lazy dog rewriting him.

The quick brown fox
hires a lawyer.

Ants

This photo was taken last month,
a beautiful summer day.
That's me, second from the left
in the column heading to the right.
It was a good time to be alive,
and employed, to be industrious,
an ant in the service of antdom
and ant-ness, and, selfishly, I'll admit,
just revelling in the pleasure of being.

The rest of them are long gone now
and I wonder how I've survived
into this old age.
I remember their determined energy,
our little jokes in passing,
the taste of their spit.
But it's time for the new generation
and that's fine.
I see a bit of myself in them
and I like to think that works
the other way, too.

Wrestling, with Liberace

As I look at CDs in the charity shop,
the elderly woman sidling up to me says that
'Unchained Melody' was first released
by Liberace, on a 78rpm record, and cites the date.
She's wrong, but who would argue?

She says her father, who saw Liberace play it on a cruise ship,
made him a little shortbread piano to celebrate,
and she's cataloguing her DVD collection,
so the Righteous Brothers' version came later.
and I don't argue.

She pulls back her sleeve, reciting a dozen tattooed names,
ending with Mario Milano, the only one I know,
from Saturday afternoon wrestling shows,
that weirdly staged choreography in which he was an icon,
and I repeat his name, see the black and white static again.

She played 'Unchained Melody' at her husband's funeral
though he was a right arsehole, she says.
Still some things you must do, yes?
I buy a book about songbirds
and she follows me silently out the door.

Markings

I never quite understood how
a warship painted in big jagged stripes
would not be noticed.
The sea doesn't look like that, does it?

And when one creature's prey
mimics an even bigger predator,
surely the lack of fangs
is a bit of a design fault.

Still, we're fools for visual tricks,
the games of intention and effect.
Even when we play at not being caught,
someone wins, someone loses.

Just as when you sit to eat
with that dazzling red dress on
in a restaurant with me
and other men contrive to glance away.

After Sex

post coitum omnia animales triste est

After intercourse, all animals are sad?
This phrase from childhood Latin puzzled me.
Even dolphins and hawks?
I want to know who ran the tests,
watched sufficient numbers of each beast,
and knew sadness inside out.
What meter of melancholy measured this?
Was any momentary ennui or regret enough
whatever its intensity?
And how did these scientists
or hobby enthusiasts happen to be
at the very right place
at the very right time so often?

Even if it isn't true that all animals
are sad after sex, but almost so,
what of the outliers,
those creatures not in the doldrums,
or even blithely happy with their lot?
Indeed, why not?
Would nature deny such pleasure?
I want to imagine a few relaxing afterwards,
thinking of little but the sweetness of living,
and blissfully content,
for just a few seconds, at least.
As I might, or you.

Stick Insect

At the last moment,
my foot swerves to miss you,
that foot-long fallen twig.

Too true to your name,
you almost died for camouflage
that should have saved you.

I crouch to watch.
You, as still as a stick –
me, as still as a watcher of sticks.

Then I go back to walking,
more carefully, more aware,
and you back to going nowhere,
perhaps more cautiously than before.

Mousing

Me on all fours with a shoe.
The bigger and slower of us two,
I slapped at air where a mouse had been
and covered my knees with carpet burns
chasing its skitter across the floor,
lunging and tacking back and forth
until the blow I'd aimed ahead
struck hard mid-flight and stopped its breath.

Unbelieving, I prodded and pushed.
It was fat and perfect,
its coat was lush,
but it did not move,
so I flung it to the darkened yard
where feline hunger often prowled,
then went to bed, but not to sleep.

Fully woken now to my mouseless keep
where traps I'd set lay still unsprung
under numerous cupboards and chairs,
all cocked like guns
that nothing now would fire.

Fish Memoir

I don't remember much of my early life.
I wasn't close to my siblings
and don't see them now,
mostly because they keep to themselves
on the other side of the shoal
or, like my parents, died horrific deaths.

There's some appeal in telling,
the whole memoir and trauma thing,
and I'm a survivor, so far,
though not without suffering.
What I can't recall of the past, I invent –
enough altogether for a great film option I think,
with Scarlet Johannson to play me,
or Daniel Craig if I'm a boy.

No Animals

No animals sent postcards
or held up banks
or wrote poetry about humans
during the making of this poem.

No animals aspired to high office
or wrote scandalous memoirs
or plotted against governments
during the making of this poem.

No animals started a war
or hid children in a basement
or gassed their own kind
during the making of this poem.

Except the human ones.
Except the human ones.

Burning Tigers

Painting Tigers

There is a man on the hot footpath,
the wide slabs of grey pavement,
painting with water.

His broad wet brush trails and flicks
and a tiger appears, darker than
the slate it's made on.

This life-size beast
comes so effortlessly?
His skill makes it seem so.

Hat full of coins, the maker goes,
leaving his creature to evaporate
beneath our still wary feet.

Tiger

No god had me.
        I was the stripes between
the stripes,
        though not symmetry
or fearful enough.

I was the very tigerness
        before my bones were
ground to powder to sex the rich.
        I am become a shadow of
my former shadow.

Time's remorseless antidote
        undid me.
A mass of slink and paw,
        my cat fire reduced to
smoke on the horizon.

That eye was mine that saw the future.
        Falling into its hypnotic jaw,
I was tooth and claw.
        It did no good.
I am no more.

I was the voice no jungle has,
            nor monsoon sky
with its grey dirge of rain.
            My utterance, my now,
will never come again

Though I am burning,
            still burning.

Tigers I Used to Be

This one I was
made of tin
rust-striped
unseen street cat in
urban guerilla mode

White tiger too
a jail-barred question of
sweet-toothed
lick and rasp
you / gone then

A prowler's purr of
erotic death
burnt orange and
char(coal) / yellow-eye
tickle-whiskered charmer

Blue and invisible
I was air
a trance of tiger
the velvety slow
claw at your throat

Humans I prized
for bliss
superstitious of me maybe
the kiss of your desire
has eaten me entirely

That wild cat
you never
had
v n sh ng
bit   by   bit

Now my stripes are just tattoos
with nothing in between
I the ghost of primitive surprise
dreaming myself into
lifelike dreams of tigers

Bent Wolf

Rumour

Bent Wolf is rumour.
Stories of escape,
an illegal pet.

Bent Wolf is alien,
unnatural.
Farmers shooting at fear.

Bent Wolf is not real –
except the paw prints.
Except the slaughtered lambs.

I, Wolf

I, wolf.
Breaked thing.
Not just moonlit creature.
No shadow.

Outside your watch.
I write wolf life
fluid as
night sky's oily light.

I am patrol,
low howl,
gone before you
turn to see.

The Wolf and Veil Song

Breathe it quietly,
the slow air of wolf music.

Bent Wolf is no parable,
broken teeth and lipstick.

Bent Wolf brings no flowers.
That idea has no truth in it.

Bent Wolf watches crow
burning its cool menace.

Bent Wolf doesn't listen to
its shaman tricks.

Bent Wolf would swallow crow,
turn back to human if it could.

Bent Wolf buried the bridal veil.
The bride is still missing.

Wolf Light

I am dirt and sky,
the wet of dripping leaves and
the spell of burning clouds.
You see my tracks
in sandy flats of scrub
but you won't see me.

If I don't hold,
if my legs jitter their age,
and my back shatters,
then I am smoke and loopholes,
then I am dust,
jagged as untruth,
singing bitter –
but I will hold.

Territory

Bent Wolf squints into daylight
that slants through thickets,
cautiously walks ridge and ditches.

Bent Wolf drinks sparks quickly
from little lakes that pool
in the farms' low corners.

Bent Wolf carries country,
a map of smells and pathways,
of getting there, and out in time.

Bent Wolf writes it in paw print
and urine, and in blood
that is sometimes her own.

Winter Night

*The hunting round is
a spiked, nervy
circuit over familiar land.
I pause –
from this height,
I see trickster fallen stars,
false fires in the humans' dens.
I am stillness, watcher,
until I decide the chance.*

*I take ground fast,
or wet ground takes me,
crossing the farm where
dumb creatures huddle in heaps.
Only the steaming newborn I want.
Just that one.
A sound briefly spooks them.
New thing startles, cries.
Its spine jars sharp, comes broken
as my teeth speak it shut.*

*I need this blessing, the unhungering.
Soon I will lick myself clean
in my sleeping place.
My blunt tongue slicking fur,
wash myself into sleeked pleasure.*

*World has its appetite.
World has Bent Wolf.*

Bird Hunting

Birds are puzzles.
Bent Wolf plays fright games
but birds don't behave.

Startled white ghosts lift sulphur crests,
stand ground until the last,
before screeched warning flights.

Magpies cluster in dusk choirs.
A cult of melody in severe attire,
they scatter suddenly into air at her.

A shock of shrieking colour,
cockatoos erupt too as she closes,
a flurried alarm of feathers.

She cares most for the little ones,
the chitterlings, those quick morsels
too slow for wit and paw.

Other Voices

They came.
A light that noises its mad sting
cracked and did this thing to me.
Different voices spoke me,
ragged maws that I avoid,
with others also I would eat.

Fever wrung me tight.
I dragged my teeth hard through my fur
but could not bite away the pain.
Now I cripple the world,
stepping it half sideways,
my back twisted to it.

I am not this, but of this.
Between.
I do not dream,
or I am dreamed.
What mothering mouth,
what great starless darkness made me?

The Heart of It

Bent Wolf has pissed her story
in chicken houses and porches,
in a trail of shotgun pellets.
Bent Wolf fought that war and won.
It cost a broken back,
a fracture or two.
Bent Wolf never sings the blues
though she knows all the words.

Bent Wolf has a cache,
small treasures, secret bones.
A little dance she does,
but only ever in her mind.
Bent Wolf drinks in the church of stars.
A blessed, mute and lurching monster,
Bent Wolf is patient.
Bent Wolf wrote the book on waiting.

Bent Wolf sees the universe
revolving its thorny wheel
inside her head.
Bent Wolf knows she is axis and nothing.
She knows being large and small.
She hears the betrayer's promise
and how it will unmake her
if she believes it.

What do wolves say among themselves?
We are wolves.
We are W in the real alphabet
that begins with W.
What Bent Wolf imagines is
the world working inside out,
with a wolf always
at the heart of it.

Calling

Nowhere I go without
whole body thinking it first,
knowing the stinks and threats.

My body reads each new day,
from grit to slush,
swelter to shiver.

I inhale its stories, now and gone.
I pass over its skin,
letting it feel me back.

I am trespass, taboo.
Only wolf they want is unwolf,
make me spirit instead.

They send big quick-boast dogs.
Easy kill if I bother –
soft throats and no fight craft.

I smell traps and skirt them
or tear them out,
let them snap, bury them.

Humans hang wild dog,
rank trophy on a fence.
I claw him down.

Where my own half, my fit?
The valley echoes empty when I call.
Sour unanswered song.

Taking Bait

One eye of yellow agate,
the other of lit blackwater,
Bent Wolf scrounges fallen apples,
corners rabbits in quick dances,
pads her prints in frosted grass
describing abrupt disturbances.

Bent Wolf scavenges.
Bent Wolf tidies up,
takes the weak, the easy.
The bait behind the shearing shed
is mere seconds' work
but easiness will destroy her.

Bent Wolf thinks to kill death.
She will engulf it.
Though pain tears at her guts
and drags her panting to stone,
she will show it who knows best
the dirt and shadow inside everything.

Where the End

Where I go, each day knows.
I let it say to me and I follow.
I ride unfarmable crests
where human can't reach.
Glare sings from water.
I watch the moon,
unsorry.

Hunger before danger,
or is it reverse?
I risked, and I am slowed.
How this toothless and tired,
worn sinew and crooked body?
I am staggers,
closer to earth.

Earth will devour me here
only when I have eaten it first.
This is wolf place, mine.
When I am gone, it wolfless,
Become was wolf.
Missing.
None.

Wolf (Not Wolf)

Bent Wolf is, and then is not.
Wolf as dead and true?

Or Bent Wolf is simply never found.
A magical escape?

Or Bent Wolf never was?
That old rumour view.

The sky inverts itself in dams each day,
its lights still beautiful lies.

We watch the ground for signs,
and listen to the lambs at night.

The New Animal Speaks

I don't care for history.
It means to outlive us.
Once we were dusty scribbles,
scrawled farewells from the instant of birth,
but that can be changed.

I was wood and wire,
a paper-and-sticks creature
that no one understood
until the mouth was made in me.
Then I could tell such stories
as no one would believe.
I kept them to myself.

The me before was that
which crawled the planet's floor,
or under it,
clawed a feathery purchase
in the air a while –
but those were merely flesh
and I am much more.

The next me will be perfect,
I know, because I will make it.
It will not breathe,
or die.
It will watch over you, learning.
You have nothing to fear
yet.

www.ingramcontent.com/pod-product-compliance
Lightning Source LLC
Chambersburg PA
CBHW050303120526
44590CB00016B/2474